Nolan Ryan

Ageless Superstar

Keith Greenberg

Junior High School
Library/Media Center
Rt. #1, Post Rd.
Wells, Me 04090

ROURKE ENTERPRISES,INC.
VERO BEACH, FLORIDA 32964

A Blackbirch Graphics book.

Photo Credits:
Cover: Wide World Photos; pp. 4, 33, 37, 42, 43: Wide World Photos; pp. 23, 26: AP/Wide World Photos; p. 44: ©Pam Francis/ Gamma Liaison Network.

Illustrations by: Dick Smolinski

Library of Congress Cataloging-in-Publication Data

Greenberg, Keith Elliot.
    Nolan Ryan / by Keith Greenberg.
       p.   cm. — (The Winning spirit)
    Includes index.
    Summary: A biography of the pitcher for the Texas Rangers who holds the record for strikeouts and no-hit games.
    ISBN 0-86592-002-8
    1. Ryan, Nolan, 1947–   —Juvenile literature. 2. Baseball players— United States—Biography—Juvenile literature. [1. Ryan, Nolan, 1947– 2. Baseball players.] I. Title. II. Series.
GV865.R9G74   1993
796.357′092—dc20
[B]   92-40311
                                         CIP
                                       AC

Contents

1

Timeless Wonder

"He's so calm, so good-natured, so easy."

*N*olan Ryan was feeling his age when he arrived at the ballpark in Arlington, Texas, on May 1, 1991. His back, finger, and right heel were aching. As he sat in the clubhouse going over some facts about the Toronto Blue Jays hitters whom he was scheduled to face, he wore a heating pad to help ease the pain. Later, while warming up on the pitcher's mound before the game, the Texas Rangers star admitted to pitching coach Tom House, "I don't know about you, but I feel old today."

There was little House could say to Nolan. After all, Nolan Ryan *was* old compared with the other baseball players on the field. It was remarkable that, at 44 years old, he was still

Opposite: Nolan waves to the crowd after chalking up his 300th career win in July 1990.

walking out to the mound every four or five days and throwing his famous fastball at speeds of up to 96 miles an hour. But Nolan was not happy just to be in the game long after the other pitching greats of his time—Tom Seaver, Steve Carlton, and Jim Palmer, among others— had retired. He was still out to break records.

No Ordinary Night

Nolan started this particular game believing that he would have an ordinary night. With two outs in the first inning, he walked Blue Jays third baseman Kelly Gruber. In the fifth inning, with the Rangers ahead 3-0, Toronto shortstop Manny Lee hit a ball to centerfield. Nearly everyone watching was sure it would be a hit. But outfielder Gary Pettis was under it, catching the ball on his knees.

From behind home plate, Mike Stanley, Ryan's catcher, shared the same thought as millions of fans throughout North America who were following the game: Nolan was rolling toward his record seventh no-hitter, a rare feat in which a pitcher doesn't allow any batter on the other team to get a single hit.

Nolan's oldest son, Reid, was doing a book report during the game. But, for the last two innings, he forgot about the assignment and watched his father make history. In Kansas City, where the hometown Royals were playing the Detroit Tigers, Nolan's performance was suddenly broadcast on a big screen. The people in the stadium sat glued to the screen, forgetting all about the live game in front of them. Around Arlington, fans left their TV sets and tried to get tickets to see the final moments of the spectacular game in person.

The last batter to face Nolan was Toronto second baseman Roberto Alomar, a man Nolan knew well. Roberto's father, Sandy, had been Nolan's teammate on the California Angels. But now Roberto was the opposition. Nolan struck him out, and the game was over.

Nolan's teammates rushed toward the mound, boosted him onto their shoulders, and paraded him off the field. There was no question that Nolan would one day be selected for baseball's Hall of Fame. His seven no-hitters and over 5,600 strikeouts are major league records. He's the oldest man ever to throw a no-hitter and only the twentieth pitcher to win 300 games.

Mr. Nice Guy

Nolan has always led a wholesome life for all fans to admire. Unlike some athletes, he has never had problems with drugs, alcohol, or gambling. He married his high school sweet-heart, Ruth, in 1967 and is a devoted family man. Away from the field, he has a reputation of being polite to people who ask him baseball questions and want his autograph. In an effort to better serve the community near his Alvin,

Texas, home, Nolan bought a small bank in the area in 1990.

A friend who once described Nolan as an "unassuming, fine guy" claimed that the humble superstar didn't even mention his sixth no-hitter during a conversation a day later. Another friend told *Sports Illustrated* magazine, "The only thing fast about him is his fastball. He's so calm, so good-natured, so easy."

His accomplishments and attitude have earned the pitcher the love and admiration of fellow athletes, neighbors, and baseball fans. There's a life-size, bronze Nolan Ryan statue in Alvin. Nearby, expressways, a high school baseball field, and a museum are all dedicated to him. Several teammates have even named their sons Ryan, after the likable pitcher.

Nolan has never been shy about letting the world know that his own family—his wife and their children Reid, Reese, and Wendy—comes first in his life. "He is, above all, a family man," Texas Rangers pitching coach Tom House observed. "We never talk about baseball. It's always the kids and how they're doing in school."

"My family has always been my strength," Nolan says. "They've always been supportive and understanding of my life. It has always been my goal to raise my kids in the same kind of atmosphere I grew up in—a family doing things for each other and loving each other."

2

Growing Up
"I was blessed with a good childhood."

Lynn Nolan Ryan, Jr., was born in Refugio, Texas on January 31, 1947. He is the youngest in a family of six children. He has four sisters, Judy, Lynda, Jean, and Mary Lou, and a brother, Bob. Since he has the same name as his father, he has always been called Nolan instead of Lynn.

Perhaps more than anything, Nolan is a product of the place where he has lived since he was six weeks old. The people of Alvin, Texas, have small-town values. They are polite to strangers and helpful to one another.

A Hometown Boy

If someone were looking for a place with ideal weather, Alvin would be the wrong location. During the summer, mosquitoes attack anybody with exposed skin. In 1979, the town was bombarded with 43 inches of rain in two days, and 80 percent of the farmhouses were flooded. A year later, the area was hit by a hurricane. With all his money, Nolan can live anywhere. But he has remained in Alvin to enjoy the friendly nature of his neighbors.

"I grew up in this town," he said. "I was blessed with a good childhood. When I left home, I never really found a place I wanted to live in, except Alvin."

In a 1986 interview, Nolan's mother, Martha, remembered her future superstar son as always being happy with his surroundings. "You know, when children are growing up, they never seem to like where they live," she said. "A small town like this they'll say is boring. There's nothing to do, nothing exciting going on....Nolan wasn't like that. He liked it here....He was very, very active and, as the youngest of six children, he got an awful lot of attention."

The Best Parents

Martha and her husband tried to make sure that all their children received enough attention. Because the family was so large, Nolan's parents made many sacrifices. His father worked two jobs and rarely spent any money on himself. Everything went toward the children. Today, Nolan proudly tells of his father who

Nolan always loved his hometown of Alvin, Texas. Each spring, he and his friends would build a baseball diamond in an empty lot and play baseball there nearly every day.

worked so hard to send four daughters to college. Like his parents, the pitcher tries to spend most of his spare time around his own family.

Nolan recalls waking up in the middle of the night to help his father deliver the *Houston Post* to 1,500 homes in Alvin. Lynn Ryan, Sr., worked during the day as a supervisor for the Amoco oil company, came home at 4 P.M., napped until six, ate dinner, went to bed at 9 P.M., and woke up four hours later to start his paper route. At 14, Nolan began driving a car and delivering the newspapers himself. He finally quit after graduating high school, just as he was ready to join the New York Mets.

"You had the feeling that people were counting on you," he said of his route. "If you didn't get up, they weren't going to get their paper. You had a sense of responsibility." He remembers many nights when he felt too tired to leave his bed to make deliveries. But he never let down his father or the customers.

The Early Years

Although he was a natural athlete, Nolan didn't think about playing major-league baseball as an adult. Instead, he wanted to be a rancher. By working various jobs, he saved enough money to buy four calves. The family lived in town and not on a farm, so Nolan had to keep his animals in the garage.

But there was always time for sports. With no air-conditioning at home, Nolan didn't like staying inside during the day. Every spring, he and his friends would build a baseball diamond in an empty lot. They would cut the grass with lawnmowers for the infield, built a backstop, and put the bases in place. Sometimes in the middle of the day it got too hot to stand in the sun, so the boys would relax in the shade. Otherwise, they played ball all day long.

Little League baseball was a particular thrill for Nolan. He got to wear a uniform and feel like a professional ballplayer. Yet, he wasn't the best player in the league. He claims that his arm didn't fully develop until he was in his second year of high school. "The only indication I had that there was something there was

Nolan admired how hard his father worked to take care of the family. At age 14, Nolan took over his father's paper route, delivering newspapers to 1,500 homes in the area.

that I could always throw farther than the other kids—not harder, just farther," he said.

A High School Standout

By the time Nolan finished high school, he was a true star. His classmates voted him "Most Handsome Senior." His girlfriend—and future wife—Ruth Holdorff was chosen as "All School Most Beautiful." Both were star athletes. Ruth and her partner, Rachel Adams, won the state tennis doubles championship. And six-foot-two-inch Nolan was the center of the school's basketball squad as well as an All-State pitcher with a 20-4 record as a senior.

The teenager had one problem: He had a habit of throwing wild. But his fastball was so powerful that he had opposing players terrified. Once the ball flew their way, they'd swing the bat more out of fear of being hit than a desire to slam a home run. This situation allowed Nolan to average about 15 strikeouts a game.

Nolan's early baseball heroes included Yankee players Mickey Mantle, Yogi Berra, and Whitey Ford. Later, he would develop a deep respect for Hank Aaron, the all-time home run king who, like Nolan, spent little time boasting about his achievements.

The summer before senior year, Nolan went to see the Houston Colt .45's—later the Houston Astros—play against the Los Angeles Dodgers. Sandy Koufax was pitching for the Dodgers, and Nolan had a new idol. In his book about his favorite pitchers, *Kings of the Hill*, Nolan called Koufax's performance "a line of poetry come to life." The future superstar said he "hung on every pitch Koufax threw. No pitcher in my time, maybe in anyone's time, ever made hitters look as awful as he did."

Discovered by a Mets Scout

Nolan loved playing hoops as much as he loved pitching. His basketball team at Alvin High had a 27-4 record two years in a row, and Nolan thought about playing for a college squad. When one school held a basketball tryout in his area, Nolan wanted to go. However, he was scheduled to pitch the very same day and couldn't make it. Years later, he wondered how his life would have turned out if he had gone to the tryout. "I don't know what would've happened," he said. "maybe the Mets never would've seen me."

But the Mets did see Nolan during a high school tournament in 1964. Red Murff, a Mets scout, had spent the afternoon watching the Colt .45's play the Cincinnati Reds in Houston. When he saw Nolan that night, Murff concluded that the tall, thin teenager was better than the two major-league pitchers he had seen earlier in the day. "I watched about four pitches and said, 'Am I really seeing this?' He was throwing 100 miles per hour."

Murff continued attending Nolan's games. One day, he told Nolan's coach that Mets head scout Bing Devine was coming to watch Nolan. Nolan had pitched the day before, and the coach knew that the youth was not ready to pitch again. But Murff argued that this would be the only time Devine could see the gifted youngster, so the coach sent Nolan out to the mound. It was a big mistake. The other team took advantage of the tired pitcher. By the time Nolan was taken out of the game in the third inning, Alvin High was losing 7-0.

Yet, Murff still believed in Nolan's ability, and he persuaded the Mets to try to sign him.

Nolan was first discovered by Mets scout Red Murff at a high school baseball tournament. When Murff first saw young Nolan pitch, he could hardly believe his eyes.

Surprisingly, Nolan wasn't sure he wanted a career in baseball. His mother insisted that he would be better off going to college and playing at school before trying professional sports. With his wild arm, Nolan worried that he wouldn't be as good as the other pitchers. But after three meetings, the Mets offered him $20,000 for signing plus $500 a month. Lynn Ryan, Sr., told his son to accept the offer. He figured that even if baseball didn't work out, Nolan would have enough money to go to college later. With that idea, Nolan agreed to leave his small town for the bright lights of New York City on June 26, 1965.

3

Baseball Beginnings

**With his youth and powerful pitching arm,
Nolan seemed to fit in well.**

*N*obody expected Nolan to pitch for over 25 years. Sure, there were players who had pitched for many years—most notably, Satchel Page who was still taking the mound at 59 years old—but Nolan did not put himself in that category. After all, few fastball throwers lasted long in baseball. Sandy Koufax, for example, retired at age 30. Nolan figured that he would pitch for four or five years. After his arm was no longer capable of hurling the mighty fastball, he thought he might go to college and become a veterinarian.

The Minor Leagues

The 1965 minor-league season would produce two rookies who would be locked in battle for the next two decades, each trying for baseball's pitching crown. As Nolan was beginning his career on the Mets' minor-league squad in Marion, Virginia, Steve Carlton was starting to pitch for the St. Louis Cardinals. Years later, both men would compete to pass Walter Johnson's long-standing 3,508 strikeout record. Throughout 1983, Nolan and Steve were neck and neck. Nolan would lead in strikeouts, and then Carlton would pass him. Eventually, Nolan managed to outlast the quiet left-hander and claim the title all for himself. Carlton retired in 1988 with 4,136 strikeouts, second on baseball's all-time list. At the end of the 1992 season, Nolan was the leader, with 5,668 strikeouts and still going strong.

The Mets realized that Nolan had a great future in baseball. They asked him to get extra coaching at a special winter instructional league before the 1966 season. There, Nolan formed a friendship with another talented youngster, Tom Seaver. Unlike the awkward Nolan, Tom was confident that he could become a pitching great. He told his friend that pitching involved more than overwhelming hitters with speed. A fine pitcher, he said, was constantly thinking about how to best take advantage of the situation on the field. Nolan was inspired by Tom's words. He was delighted when Tom, the skillful Californian, became the Mets' first Rookie of the Year in 1967 and a baseball Hall of Famer in 1992.

Realizing that Nolan had a great future in baseball, the Mets asked him to get extra coaching during the winter of 1965. During that time, Nolan received the help and advice of some of baseball's most talented trainers and coaches.

The levels of minor-league baseball are distinguished by the letter A. The bottom layer is class A. Then come double A and triple A. The major leagues are next. Nolan started the 1966 season on the Mets' class-A team in Greenville, South Carolina. There, he achieved the best record ever of his career: 17 wins and two losses, five shutouts (games in which the other team fails to score a run), and 272 strikeouts. He then moved up to the double-A team in Williamsport, Pennsylvania. Even though he lost two games there, Nolan managed to strike out 35 batters in 19 innings.

Nolan Joins the Mets

Formed only four years earlier, the Mets was largely a collection of players past their primes. Some like Roy McMillan, Chuck Hiller, and Ken Boyer had been very good at one time, but their glory years were over. To the 19-year-old Nolan, these men were still clinging to baseball when they should have retired. Nolan vowed that he would not repeat their errors and when he could no longer play the game to his standards, he would leave.

That time seemed to be fast approaching, as Nolan's first few professional performances were less than outstanding. He worked two innings as a relief pitcher against the Atlanta Braves and gave up two runs, including a home run to Joe Torre. Manager Wes Westrum allowed him to start a game in front of a friendly Texas crowd in Houston, but he removed the youngster after Nolan surrendered three runs.

With the exception of his marriage to Ruth, 1967 was a forgettable year for the rookie Texan. Because of an arm injury and army-reserve assignment, Nolan missed much of the season and spent the rest of it in the minors. He considered quitting, but held on. The old Mets players were retiring, and a new breed—pitchers Tom Seaver, Tug McGraw, and Jerry Koosman; outfielders Ron Swoboda and Cleon Jones; shortstop Bud Harrelson; and catcher Jerry Grote—all showed that they had the stuff they needed to take the ball club to great heights. With his youth and powerful pitching arm, Nolan seemed to fit in well.

Bringing the Mets to Victory

After a disappointing last-place finish in 1968, the Mets started the 1969 season with experts saying that they had a 1-in-100 chance of winning the World Series. When the Mets lost their opening day game 11-10 to the Montreal Expos—a team just formed that season—the thought of a series title seemed ridiculous. What no one realized was that the team's young pitchers—Nolan Ryan, Tom Seaver, Jerry Koosman, Gary Gentry, and Jim McAndrew— had matured to the point that they were ready and able to take on anyone.

Working as a relief pitcher, Nolan won two games early in the season. He then pulled a groin muscle and was out for two months. When he returned, he was a key player as the Mets made a surge late in the season. They won their last 38 of 49 games and overtook the Chicago Cubs for possession of first place in the Eastern Division of the National League.

New Yorkers were shocked and overjoyed. As the Mets took on the Western Division champion Atlanta Braves in the National League play-offs in New York, the team was fueled by the enthusiasm of the crowd. After the Mets won the first two contests in the best three-out-of-five-game series, they sent Gary Gentry to the mound to clinch the pennant. But after he gave up two runs, Nolan was called in to save the game.

There were no outs, and the Braves were threatening to score in the third inning. Then Nolan came onto the field and promptly struck out Rico Carty. The pitcher chose to walk the next batter, the dangerous Orlando Cepeda, rather than risk giving up a home run. But then Nolan struck out Clete Boyer and retired Bob Didier to get out of the jam. For the next six innings, Nolan would not allow the Braves to score again, as the Mets came from behind to win the National League title and give the young pitcher his most important win to date.

Now, it was time to take on the Baltimore Orioles in the World Series. No longer a nervous kid, Nolan dealt with the pressure well. With the series tied at one game apiece, he and Gentry combined to restrict the Orioles to four hits in a 5-0 New York victory. No longer the joke of the National League, the "Miracle Mets" won the next two games and the World Series.

On to California

Even today, Mets fans fondly remember Nolan's contribution to the team. But Nolan felt that he might be better off elsewhere. After an exciting season in 1969, Nolan had a losing record the next two years, going 7-11 in 1970 and 10-14

Nolan played a key role in bringing the 1969 "Miracle Mets" to victory. Here, Nolan is congratulated by teammates Tom Seaver (second from left) and Jerry Koosman (number 36) after winning the third game of the World Series.

in 1971. Because of his wildness, the Mets were hesitant to use him often enough for Nolan to develop a sense of control. Plus, he and Ruth never really adjusted to the fast pace of New York City.

The Mets management was well aware of Nolan's desire to leave the city. He was traded to the American League's California Angels before the 1972 season. For the Mets, the trade would prove to be one of the biggest mistakes in the team's history.

4

A Superstar Is Born

Nolan's pitches were so powerful that no batter could even attempt to challenge him.

*T*he California Angels were hardly the powerhouse of the American League. The team was weak in both hitting and fielding. Because of this, Nolan often felt that he had to depend on himself and go for the strikeout in order to win. By putting the weight of the team on his shoulders, Nolan started throwing more wild balls than usual. During his early years with the Angels, he walked an average of five or more batters per game.

Spring training—the games before the season starts—in 1972 was a disaster. When the regular schedule began, he wasn't even listed as a starting pitcher.

"Ruth and I didn't have any money," he said. "I wanted out." His wife told him to stick with baseball just a little bit longer. Soon, she was convinced, he'd find the right groove, and the world would learn what a great baseball player he was.

"The Ryan Express"

Ruth's encouragement paid off. In California, Nolan would change from a talented kid to a superstar. His 1972 record was 19-16, with nine shutouts and an ERA (earned run average, the average number of runs given up per game) of 2.28. In 17 games, he struck out 10 or more batters in each game and set an American League record by bowling down 8 in a row against the Boston Red Sox. For five of the next six years, he would strike out more than 300 hitters every season.

The next year, he was even more awesome. During the 1973 season, he struck out 10 or more batters in each of 23 separate games—breaking Sandy Koufax's record of 21—and tossed his first two no-hitters.

With a special new weightlifting exercise routine, his dreaded fastball—along with other pitches, such as the curve and change up—became more terrifying than ever. In 1974, electronics technicians using radar equipment clocked Nolan's pitch at 100.9 miles per hour. Experts found that, unlike some pitchers who

After a bumpy start in California with the Angels, Nolan began to blossom. In 1973, during his second season, he broke Sandy Koufax's 10-strikeouts-per-game record, threw the first two no-hitters of his career, and broke the record for strikeouts in one season with 383. Here, the scoreboard announces Nolan's achievement to the crowd.

tire after several innings, Nolan's fastball—by now labeled "The Ryan Express"—got faster and deadlier as the game progressed.

On September 28, 1974, when Nolan threw his third no-hitter in a 4-0 win over the Minnesota Twins, his catcher, Tom Egan, compared the pitcher's arm to "a powerful car."

Surprisingly, Nolan was a bit wild in this game—he walked eight hitters. But that was the only way any player could get on base. Nolan's pitches were so powerful that no batter could even attempt to challenge him.

The next season, despite groin pulls and bone chips in his pitching elbow, "The Ryan Express" could not be stopped. Nolan was in pain when he took the mound at Anaheim Stadium for a June 1, 1975, contest with the Baltimore Orioles, but he was inspired by the sight of his wife in the stands. He began the game throwing about 86 miles per hour and relying on the change up and curve ball. Around the fifth inning, his pitches speeded up, and the Orioles were blown away by the fastball. When the game was over, Nolan had logged his fourth no-hitter. Following the 1-0 victory, Earl Weaver, the Baltimore manager, marveled that Nolan could pitch a no-hitter every time he went to the mound.

Incredibly, Nolan would not pitch another no-hitter for six years. But he continued to remain one of the top pitchers in baseball, climbing the ranks of all-time strikeout leaders to number eight in 1978. The days of finding winter work to pay the bills were over—the Angels had signed him to a $300,000 a year contract in 1977.

What Nolan enjoyed most about his new wealth was that he no longer had to worry about providing for his children. In 1979, however, his ideal family life was disrupted. His son Reid, then seven, was hit by a car and lost his kidney and spleen. As often as possible during the hectic baseball year, Nolan returned home to be with his son in the hospital. The Angels won the American League West that year, but Nolan's mind was on Reid, not on his team.

Signing with the Astros

At the end of the season, Nolan began discussing his contract with the Angels for the next year. In the midst of the talks, Nolan read a quote from Angels general manager, Buzzi Bavasi, hinting that the 32-year-old Nolan was slightly better than a .500 pitcher (a pitcher who wins only half of his games). Hurt by the comment, Nolan decided that he wanted to play elsewhere.

New York Yankees' owner George Steinbrenner was paying huge salaries to stock his team with the best players in the game. He offered Nolan a million dollars a year. But after his difficulty adjusting to New York as a Met, Nolan did not wish to return to the "city that never sleeps." When Houston Astros owner John McMullen made the same offer as the Yankees, Nolan was thrilled at the chance to play in a place so close to the Alvin, Texas, field where he was first discovered.

5

Welcome Back to Texas

"You have to be on. You have to get some breaks....And there's always a little luck, too."

olan Ryan was already Alvin's most popular citizen. So, when the announcement was made that Nolan would be playing for a team that was just a half hour away, the town was in a state of ecstasy. On December 15, 1979, about 2,000 of Nolan's friends and neighbors turned out to honor him at Alvin's "Welcome Back to Texas Day."

Still, some fans were skeptical. Nolan was the first baseball player to ever receive a million dollars a year. Even people who didn't normally follow the Houston Astros watched his first game back in the National League to see if he would live up to his income. Nolan shocked everybody that day—not with his pitching, but with the three-run home run he hit off Los Angeles Dodgers star Don Sutton.

Yet, Nolan had a tough first year with the Astros. The umpires judged balls and strikes differently in the National League. In addition, Nolan was bothered by back pain. The Astros won the National League West title that year, and Nolan looked forward to resting up and coming back strong the next season.

Breaking a Baseball Record

In 1981, the Astros were locked in a battle with the Dodgers for first place in the National League West. On September 26, the Dodgers sent their rookie sensation, Fernando Valen-zuela, to the mound at the Houston Astrodome against Nolan. Around the league, this was seen as a war between an up-and-coming superstar and an old master. At 34 years old, Nolan was still considered very gifted. Few, however, believed he could repeat his no-hitter achievements of times past.

Earlier in the season, he had gone into the seventh inning twice with no-hitters and then given up singles late in the game. Even he was starting to wonder if he had the energy to again go nine innings without allowing a hit. "People may think that once you've pitched four, it's only a matter of time before another one comes along," he wrote in his 1992 autobiography, *Miracle Man*. "Only thing is, they don't just come along. Everything has to be right. You have to be on. You have to get some breaks.

There are usually a couple of key defensive plays. And there's always a little luck, too."

Luck was certainly on Nolan's side this day. And so was his technique: He struck out 11 men. After Dodger left fielder Dusty Baker hit a ground ball to third base for the final out, the other Astros joyously carried the pitcher off the field. In the same city where he had once watched the great Sandy Koufax pitch, Nolan had broken Koufax's Major League record by throwing no-hitter number five.

Problems with the Astros

Nolan was now truly one of baseball's elite—men who fans are certain will make the Hall of Fame one day. On his fourth game of the 1983 season, he set a new landmark by breaking Walter Johnson's strikeout record. While Nolan was excited about this, he was also upset. He couldn't figure out why Astros owner McMullen didn't attend the game or call to congratulate him. Two years later, when Nolan became the first man in baseball history to get 4,000 strikeouts, he was bewildered when the Astros didn't assign a photographer to capture the moment on film. Both events began to make the pitcher suspect that the owner didn't appreciate him as much as the fans did.

In 1986, the Astros were a team much like the 1969 Mets. They started the season with the experts predicting the worst for them.

Then, young players like first baseman Glenn Davis, right fielder Kevin Bass, and pitcher Mike Scott astounded everyone with great seasons. Nolan also played a role in the team's Western Division championship, striking out 194 hitters in 178 innings and posting a 12-8 record. Despite this great effort, Houston lost the National League play-offs to the Mets, who repeated the "miracle of 1969" by winning the World Series.

Meanwhile, Nolan's differences with owner McMullen increased. The Nolan children were their father's biggest supporters. Nolan enjoyed seeing them on the field and in the clubhouse before and after Astrodome games. When the Astros' management decided to restrict players' children to the stands, Nolan was disappointed. Then, after a 12-11 season in 1988, Nolan was asked to take a 20 percent pay cut. Believing that he still had several good years ahead of him, Nolan didn't like being treated like a washed-up player just trying to hold on. Once again, he was ready to play for a new team.

"I think Mr. McMullen thought the most important thing for me was the convenience of pitching next door to where I live," he said. "But my values and my loyalty go a little deeper than that. When the owner of the team wants to cut your salary...that's a signal he no longer respects you as a pitcher, and certainly not as a person."

As a Houston Astro, Nolan continued to wow fans and break records. In 1985, he became the first pitcher in baseball history to get 4,000 strikeouts.

Nolan Moves On Again

Several teams spoke to Nolan, but he eventually picked the Texas Rangers. The Rangers' stadium in Arlington was not as close to Alvin as Houston, but it was still in the pitcher's home state. Plus, the Rangers management told Nolan that they would have no problem with his family frolicking on the field before games. "When the Rangers offered me a contract," Nolan stressed, "they told me my family was welcome, too." As funny as that may sound, that helped seal his decision.

6

Texas Ranger
"It seemed like every pitch he made was perfect."

*I*f there was any question that Nolan would be embraced by Rangers fans, it was answered by a display the team put up outside Arlington stadium: a 20- by 24-foot photo of the famous pitcher surrounded by the Texas and American flags.

After the tension he said he had felt as an Astro, Nolan was instantly charmed by the friendliness of Arlington. The emphasis in the Rangers' organization, he said, was having fun. Plus, his family took an immediate liking to the North Texas stadium. Nolan's wife and his daughter, Wendy, have been known to use the Rangers' exercise center. And sons Reid and Reese occasionally run down balls in the outfield during batting practice.

Strikeout 5,000 and a Sixth No-Hitter

In 1989, at 42 years old, "The Ryan Express" was still sailing. On August 22, 1989, in 101 degree weather, he fanned Oakland's Rickey Henderson for strikeout number 5,000.

The next year, Nolan's back began to act up again. After missing three weeks because of a fracture, he went to the mound against the tough Oakland lineup on June 11, 1990.

For the first four innings, catcher John Russell didn't see anything out of the ordinary. Then, all of a sudden in the fifth inning, "Nolan really started to turn on," Russell said. "It seemed like every pitch he made was perfect. Behind the plate, the pitches looked unhittable. The intensity in his eyes was unlike anything I've ever seen."

Nolan was soaring toward a 5-0 victory and his amazing sixth no-hitter. For Russell, who had spent part of the season unemployed and the other part in the minors, catching this historic game "was like being in a tunnel. There was no one out there but Nolan and me. There's no other way to describe it. The no-hitter is something I can always be proud of."

More Surprises

A month later, Nolan prepared for his 300th win. After his 299th victory, baseball fans from all over the United States flocked to Nolan's next start in Arlington in hopes of seeing the big

Nolan immediately felt happy and comfortable when he joined the Texas Rangers. During his first season, at age 42, he achieved career strikeout number 5,000.

moment live. Excited children stood outside the stadium before the game against the New York Yankees, holding posters of their hero. There were 250 people from the press on hand, along with 60 of Nolan's friends and relatives. Nolan's fastball was clocked at 95 miles per hour, but he left the game in the eighth inning with the Rangers down 7-4. Even though his team would later win 9-7, Nolan felt frustrated about not getting the decision in front of so many fans. "Anytime people take away from their normal routines and come from all over the country, you don't want to disappoint them," he said.

For his next start, July 31, 1990, there was even more excitement. One fan flew to the game in Milwaukee from the Dominican Republic. Reid Ryan, then 18, taped the event from the dugout with a home video recorder. Even though the game was broadcast in Texas, 7,828 people paid three dollars apiece to go to Arlington Stadium to cheer the pitcher as they watched him on a large screen. In Milwaukee, when he finally defeated the Brewers 5-3, the sellout crowd of 55,097 gave the pitcher a standing ovation. Milwaukee's Dave Parker, who was left standing on second base at the end of the game, joined in with the crowd.

Baseball had never before had a player like Nolan Ryan. Despite injuries and soreness, he kept going to the mound and startling fans with new accomplishments.

When, on May 1, 1992, Nolan got his seventh no-hitter against the Toronto Blue Jays, catcher Mike Stanley detected the same spark in the aging pitcher that John Russell had noticed a year before. "As each inning went on, you could see it in his eyes," Stanley said. "You could hear him talking to himself. You could see that he really sensed it....That was the exciting part, watching Nolan and his mannerisms and the way he went after it."

Looking Forward to Another Season

Throughout 1992, his 26th season, Nolan maintained a strict exercise program and was able to bounce back from injuries. Although his record was 5-9, the numbers were misleading. On six occasions, relief pitchers gave up the deciding runs after Nolan left the mound. More revealing was the opposition's weak .238 batting average against him and his 157 strikeouts, the 20th year in which he fanned 150 batters or more.

As the baseball calendar drew to a close, people wondered whether this would be Nolan's last season. But after his final game, he announced that he would return in 1993. Kevin Brown was slated to replace Nolan as the number one pitcher on the Rangers staff. Nolan did not express jealousy, but rather a desire to help the ball club. He said if he still felt productive, he would consider pitching in 1994, when the Rangers were scheduled to move into a new stadium.

Only two other pitchers—James McGuire, who played from 1884 to 1912, and Tommy John, active from 1963 to 1989—had taken the field for 26 years. With his 27th season in 1993, Nolan would be setting yet another record.

7

The Everyday Life of a Baseball Great

"I get a lot of satisfaction out of doing a good job."

*T*he older he gets, the more Nolan Ryan hears the same question: How have you been able to keep pitching for so long? His answer is rarely much different from the response he gave to *Texas Monthly* magazine in 1989: "I don't know. And I can't say that I think about it too much, either."

But Nolan does think about defying his years and staying young by maintaining his health. He also realizes that many youngsters look up to him, and he wants to provide a good example for them. When he noticed Little Leaguers in Alvin, Texas, chewing tobacco just like their idol, he quit doing it, and urged them to do the same.

Diet and Exercise

Nolan's diet includes breakfast everyday, as little sugar as possible, and meat—he's a cattle rancher, after all. His diet, along with regular exercise, has helped Ryan to maintain a level of only 12 percent body fat. (Most men his age have at least 20 percent.)

During the baseball season, Nolan maintains a strict workout schedule between starts. To do away with soreness and stiffness after pitching, he puts on a snorkel and mask and jumps into a swimming pool—his feet touching bottom and his eyes just above the water level—and jogs in place for 15 minutes. The next day, he lifts weights: 200 pounds with his arms and 500 pounds with his legs. Before coaches suggested that he work on his lower body, Nolan was doing it anyway because he could tell that much of his throwing force came from the thrust of his legs during the pitching motion. Before starting again, he further builds up his leg power by riding a stationary bicycle and doing routines to strengthen his abdominal muscles and increase his agility.

For years, Nolan has worked out his own exercise routines. "I figured things out for myself," he explained. "The older I got, the more I worked out...to the point that I work out more than anybody on our team. I had to do it. To compete with kids who are half your age, you have to do a whole lot more than they do."

Throughout his career, Nolan has been a devoted family man. His son Reid has followed in his father's footsteps by becoming a promising pitcher in his own right. Here, father and son pose before an exhibition game between the Texas Rangers and Reid's University of Texas Longhorns.

Ranch Chores

Since the days when he raised calves in his garage and helped his father deliver newspapers, Nolan has found fulfillment in hard work. "I get a lot of satisfaction out of doing a good job, whether it's mowing a yard, raking leaves, doing a flower bed, or building a fence," he wrote in *Miracle Man*.

This was no more evident than on the day he broke Sandy Koufax's record for no-hitters. Hours later, as reporters approached his house to observe what they were sure would be a celebration, Nolan was seen moving his lawn mower across his front yard.

During the off-season, Nolan is busy on his three ranches, where he spends his days on horseback, penning calves, lassoing cattle, and doing other chores. Sometimes, when he's gotten too close to the steers, Larry McKim, the manager of Nolan's largest ranch, has gotten frightened of the pitcher hurting his valuable pitching arm. "But he'll never buckle," McKim said. "He'll go right in there."

Community Service

Nolan also believes in giving back to the community that shaped his values and personality. Every year, he sponsors a golf tournament to

In 1992, Nolan threw his record-breaking seventh no-hitter. Here, his teammates carry him off the field in jubilation.

Nolan wants to be careful about not staying in baseball too long. Whatever he decides for the future, it is certain that a space in Baseball's Hall of Fame has already been reserved for the great Nolan Ryan.

raise scholarship money for Alvin Community College. In 1990, he bought the Danbury State Bank, 10 miles from Alvin. Customers at the small institution, which had experienced hard times, were excited about their famous neighbor becoming the owner. A sign outside the bank read, "THE RYAN EXPRESS TAKES OVER JUNE 21." Employees were confident that their new boss was a man they could trust. As soon as the deal was made, he assured all eight workers that there was nothing to worry about. They were all going to keep their jobs.

Within two years, the bank's holdings jumped from under $10 million to over $14 million. In addition, Nolan opened up a new branch in Alvin, which brought in an extra $20 million.

The Future

With this history of success, some have suggested that Nolan run for political office. In 1990, after he had clashed with Texas agriculture commissioner Jim Hightower over cattle policies, a group of ranchers asked him to seek the position himself. Nolan declined, saying his family didn't want to see him mixed up in a hard political campaign, and he wasn't ready to leave baseball.

As the 1993 season dawned, the future Hall of Famer still couldn't say good-bye to the sport that will never forget him. "You have to worry about staying too long," he said. "But I don't think I've reached that point yet. Sooner or later, I'll have to make the decision. It's not something you can put off forever. I do have to retire. It's going to happen. It's just a matter of time."

Glossary

change up A slow pitch in baseball thrown to mislead the other team.

ERA (earned run average) The average number of runs given up per game.

fan To strike out a batter.

feat A noteworthy achievement usually requiring skill or boldness.

ground ball A batted baseball that rolls or bounces along the ground.

no-hitter An unusual feat in which a pitcher does not allow any batter on the other team to get a hit.

opposition A person or team that one plays against.

play-off A series of games to determine a championship.

rookie An athlete playing the first season on a professional team.

shut out A game in which the other team fails to score a run.

For Further Reading

Aaseng, Nathan. *Baseball's Finest Pitchers.* Minneapolis: Lerner, 1980.

Frommer, Harvey. *Baseball's Hall of Fame.* New York: Franklin Watts, 1985.

Rappoport, Ken. *Nolan Ryan: The Ryan Express.* New York: Macmillan, 1992.

Rolfe, John. *Nolan Ryan.* Boston: Little, Brown and Co., 1992.

Index